Radio Waves

Nicolas Brasch

Radio Waves

Rigby Heinemann
a division of Reed International Books Australia Pty Ltd
22 Salmon Street, Port Melbourne, Victoria 3207
World Wide Web   http://www.rigby.com.au
Email   info@hi.com.au

Offices in Sydney, Brisbane, Perth and Adelaide. Associated
companies, branches and representatives throughout the world.

Designed by Caz Brown
Photographic research by Lizzie Whyte
Edited by Sarah Russell

Film supplied by Type Scan, Adelaide
Printed by Dah Hua Printing Press Co., Hong Kong

National Library of Australia
ISBN 0 7312 3271 2

Acknowledgments for photographs: © ABC Document Archives pp. 23, 26;
© ABC Radio p. 20; © Australian Picture Library p. 21; © Coo-ee Picture Library
pp. 5, 7, 12; © Herald and Weekly Times Photographic Collection p. 29; © Image
Library/State Library of New South Wales p. 11; © Kino Studio Photo Archive
pp. 8, 10, 17; © National Library of Australia pp. 25, 27; © State Library of Victoria
p. 15; © Triple M Radio p. 19.

Contents

What Is Radio?

Radio waves

Radio is the transmission of signals from one place to another through the use of radio waves. The discovery of radio waves meant that messages could be sent long distances without the need for wires. That is why radios were first called wirelesses.

Radio waves carry sound signals from one place to another. They are invisible but are all around us, and they travel at the speed of light. Many things must happen for the sounds you hear through your radio to reach you. First, the voice or music goes through a microphone and is turned into an **electrical current**. A **transmitter** then turns this current into a radio wave. The wave travels around until it hits a radio aerial on top of a radio tuned to the right **frequency**. A receiver in the radio turns the wave back into a sound.

An old wireless.

Inventors

The person usually given the most credit for the invention of the radio is Guglielmo Marconi, an Italian scientist. However, other people were also involved in the development of the radio.

In 1864, a Scottish physicist (an expert in physics) called James Clerk Maxwell produced mathematical evidence that radio waves existed. A German physicist called Heinrich Hertz then conducted experiments in 1888 that proved Maxwell's theory was correct. But, in 1895, it was Marconi who became the first person to send an actual message using a transmitter and receiver that he had built. In 1901, he sent a message across the Atlantic Ocean to

This illustration shows Marconi demonstrating wireless transmission in London in 1896.

the United States. Marconi's messages were not actual voices but **Morse Code**.

Other major figures in the development of radio were John Ambrose Fleming and Lee De Forest who developed instruments to transmit the human voice. Also significant was Reginald Aubrey Fessenden, whose voice was the first to be successfully transmitted by radio waves.

Today, it is just a matter of flicking a switch to hear a voice or music, but it is interesting to think about the work and effort that went into making radio so simple.

From ship to shore

In 1910, a murderer called Dr Crippen left London just before the police came to arrest him. The police had no idea where he had gone and issued a **warrant** for his arrest. Dr Crippen had boarded a ship bound for Canada. The ship's captain became suspicious of Crippen's behaviour, and because he had read the police warrant, he used the ship's radio to contact police. Dr Crippen was then arrested in Canada. This was the first time radio was used in a murder investigation.

History of Radio in Australia

Early days

Australia was not far behind the rest of the world in the early days of the development of radio. Professor William Bragg demonstrated Marconi's radio technology in Adelaide in 1897, and then went to England to meet Marconi and learn more about wireless transmission.

Early radio broadcasts were broadcast, transmitted and picked up by amateur radio enthusiasts. Many of these enthusiasts worked as radio operators during World War I. It was in this war that communication by radio became an important part of war for the first time.

First official station

It was not until 1923 that radio stations were first licensed by the government. Licences were issued so that the government could have some control over how radio waves were being used. The first official station was 2SB, which began broadcasting at 8:00 p.m. on 13 November 1923. Early stations operated on a **subscription** basis. On payment of a fee, people received a radio that was set on the frequency of the stations they had subscribed to. The Australian Broadcasting Commission (ABC) began broadcasting on 1 July 1932.

Golden era

The importance of radio increased during World War II. For the first time, Australians could hear, rather than just read, reports from the battle fronts. The years after World War II are considered to be radio's golden era. Radio drama became very popular. Families would

Children's hour at 3LO on Friday, a popular radio program for children in the 1940s.

sit around the radio together, much like families watch television nowadays. The most popular radio dramas were "Blue Hills", "The Lawsons" and "Dad and Dave".

Australian children were not forgotten. They had their own club and radio program called the "Argonauts Club". The Argonauts Club ran for thirty years, from 1941 to 1971, and over 50 000 Australian children became members of the club during that time.

When television was introduced to Australia in 1956, many people suggested that radio would no longer be popular. However, many of the most popular shows continued to be successful, and even today radio and television happily exist side by side.

Power of radio

One of the most famous radio broadcasts of all time took place in the United States on 30 October 1938. The actor and director Orson Welles broadcast a radio drama of H. G. Wells' book, *War of the Worlds*, in which Earth is invaded by Martians. Unfortunately, many people believed that they were hearing a news broadcast and that the invasion was really happening. They fled their homes in panic and tried to find somewhere safe to hide. From then on, no-one questioned the power of radio.

Australia's Radio Industry

Unlike Australia's television industry, there are few national radio stations. Most stations broadcast to a particular city or country area. The Australian radio industry is controlled by the Australian Broadcasting Authority, which was set up in 1992. Anyone wishing to start up a radio station has to apply to the Australian Broadcasting Authority for a licence.

This is the logo for Triple M, Brisbane.

Types of radio stations

There are three types of radio stations in Australia: government-funded stations, such as the ABC and SBS; commercial stations, such as Fox and Triple M; and public radio, such as 3RPH.

Government-funded stations

There are more than fifty ABC radio stations around Australia, including Triple J and Radio National, both of which are heard virtually everywhere in Australia. Most of the other ABC stations serve a particular city or **regional** area. SBS broadcasts foreign language programs around Australia.

Commercial stations

There are about 245 commercial radio stations in Australia. The vast majority of them are music stations. Commercial radio stations depend on advertising to survive. The more people they can get to listen to them, the more money they can charge for companies to advertise on their station. That is why **ratings** are very important to commercial stations.

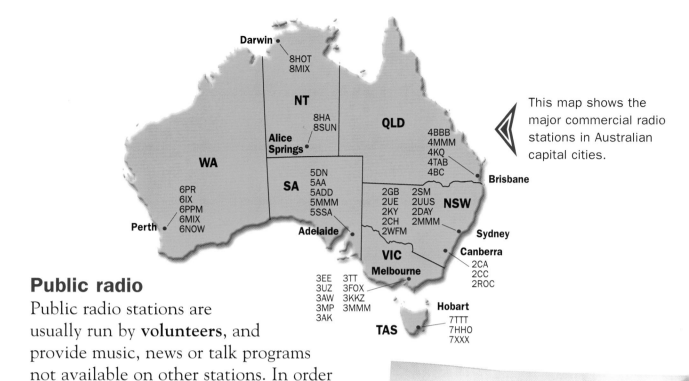

Darwin
8HOT
8MIX

NT

8HA
8SUN

Alice
Springs

QLD

4BBB
4MMM
4KQ
4TAB
4BC

Brisbane

WA

6PR
6IX
6PPM
6MIX
6NOW

Perth

SA

5DN
5AA
5ADD
5MMM
5SSA

Adelaide

2GB   2SM
2UE   2UUS
2KY   2DAY
2CH   2MMM
2WFM

NSW

Sydney

Canberra
2CA
2CC
2ROC

VIC

Melbourne

3EE   3TT
3UZ   3FOX
3AW   3KKZ
3MP   3MMM
3AK

TAS

Hobart
7TTT
7HHO
7XXX

This map shows the major commercial radio stations in Australian capital cities.

Public radio

Public radio stations are usually run by **volunteers**, and provide music, news or talk programs not available on other stations. In order to survive, they depend on donations from companies, organisations and listeners. Many public stations broadcast to a particular audience, such as blind people.

AM or FM?

Except for a brief period in the 1950s, radio stations in Australia operated solely on the **AM** band until 1976. This was because the **FM** band was reserved for television transmission. The ABC began transmitting on the FM band in 1976, while the first commercial FM station was 3EON, which began in 1980. Sounds carried on AM waves travel further than on FM but are not as clear, so most AM stations are talk stations, and most FM stations play music.

Investigating complaints

If a person has a complaint about something they have heard on a radio station, they should complain to the radio station involved. If the radio station does not respond to their complaint satisfactorily, they can take their complaint to the Australian Broadcasting Authority. If the Australian Broadcasting Authority considers that the radio station has behaved in an inappropriate manner, they can set conditions on the radio station's licence, which means a similar complaint could result in the station losing its right to broadcast.

How a Radio Station Works

All of the news, information and music that can be heard on the radio comes from a studio. At most radio stations, the studio is divided into two sections. There is a room where the presenter or disc jockey sits, and there is a control room that contains most of the broadcasting equipment and is where the technical staff are based. The two sections are separated by a glass panel, so that the presenter and the technical staff can see each other.

The radio presenter sits in a soundproof room.

Presenter's room

The presenter's room is soundproof, which means that outside noises cannot get in. When the presenter talks, he or she does so into a microphone. A red light indicates when the microphone is open, and that means that the presenter can be heard by an audience. This stops embarrassing moments, such as swearing or private chat, going to air.

Control room

The control room is where the sound being broadcast is controlled. Several people may be working in the control room at any one time. A producer will give instructions to the presenter by computer or through headphones. A studio manager will control the level and quality of the sound being broadcast. There may also be an assistant producer running errands and taking telephone calls from listeners.

One of the earlier trucks used as an outside broadcast van by the ABC.

Small radio stations

Smaller radio stations may have only a one-room studio. In this case, one person is generally in charge of everything. Their job may be to broadcast, to control the sound quality, take telephone calls, and play music and advertisements, all at the same time.

Program planning

All radio programs are planned in advance. The producer and presenter have a **running sheet** that sets out the order in which interviews, music, advertisements and news are to be broadcast. The time set down for each item is strictly followed. If too long is spent on one item, other items will have to be shortened or left out.

Outside broadcasts

Some radio stations have outside broadcast vans, which are vehicles that contain a mobile studio. This enables the station to broadcast from locations anywhere outside the regular studio. The most popular outside broadcasts are those from sporting venues. Several outside broadcast vans may be found at a football ground during winter. Some of the most unusual locations for outside broadcasts have been hospitals, prisons, on top of the Sydney Harbour Bridge, and on board a Melbourne tram.

Who Does What?

Station manager

The person in charge of a radio station is the station manager. He or she makes sure that the station obeys the conditions of its licence and attracts enough revenue from advertisers, sponsors or the government to run effectively.

A journalist gathers information for a story.

Programming

A program manager decides the type of programs that a station broadcasts. They select the disc jockeys and presenters they think will prove most popular with the audience they want to attract. If a radio station is not getting high ratings, the program manager will make changes to increase ratings.

News

The news room is responsible for gathering and broadcasting news items. A news director decides which stories are most important and sends the station's journalists to interview people. Journalists then write their stories and record them onto tapes. A newsreader reads the news from a script written by themselves or by a writer, and the journalists' tapes are played at the appropriate moments.

Marketing

The marketing department is responsible for ideas to attract listeners to the station. They suggest new competitions or try to get articles about their presenters and programs published in newspapers and magazines.

Sales

The sales department is responsible for attracting advertisers. Advertising representatives visit companies, trying to convince them to advertise on the radio station. Many radio stations will help make advertisements. They will employ **copywriters** to write the advertisements, **voice-over artists** to read the advertisements and musicians to write jingles.

Writing jingles

A jingle is a catchy tune designed to catch the attention of the listener. It is generally used to help advertise a product but may also be used as a radio station **call-sign**. Jingles are written by musicians and must fulfil three criteria. They should suit the product being advertised; they should be short and catchy so people hum them and recognise them; and they should help sell the product. Perhaps the two most famous Australian jingles are those written for Vegemite™ and Aeroplane Jelly™.

Producer

Although disc jockeys and presenters get the most publicity, the most important person involved in the production of a radio program is the producer. The producer decides a program's content, arranges interviews, organises the order in which the program **segments** will be broadcast and makes sure that the program runs smoothly. If an interviewee does not turn up on time, the producer directs the presenter how to proceed.

Broadcasting Music

Although we think of the early days of radio as being dominated by dramas and quiz shows, the fact is that, like today, the majority of radio programs broadcast music. Before rock and roll came along in the 1950s, opera, classical music and popular songs filled the airwaves. Two of the most popular programs were "Music for the People" and "Opera for the People", made in the 1940s by Hector and Dorothy Crawford, who later produced some of Australia's best-known television programs.

Music for the young

In the 1950s, teenagers began listening to radio like never before. Top 40 charts and request shows became popular. More and more radio stations began programming music for young people because it meant larger audiences, which meant advertisers would be willing to pay more to have their products promoted. The introduction of television to Australia in 1956 meant radio stations had to rethink their programming strategies. Families preferred to sit around and watch dramas, quizzes and variety shows on television, rather than listen to them on the radio. However, the fact that people could listen to music while they moved around the house or were supposed to be doing homework helped those stations that played music to survive.

The 1950s and 1960s saw radios become smaller and smaller, so they were no longer just to be listened to at home. Young people could carry them down the street and to the beach, listening to the stations that played the music they enjoyed. Radios also began to be fitted into cars at the time that it first became possible for young people to save up and buy a car.

 Young people took smaller, more portable radios to the beach.

Television

Television stations saw what was happening on radio and began making music programs. The most famous ones in Australia were "Bandstand" and "6 O'clock Rock". Instead of being competitors, television and radio stations helped one another. They promoted new and popular acts that the fans couldn't get enough of.

Ahoy! Pirates!

While American and Australian radio stations were quick to recognise the benefits of playing rock music, the only radio broadcaster in Britain was the government-owned BBC (British Broadcasting Corporation). The BBC introduced the music of groups such as the Beatles and the Rolling Stones to the British public. But **pirate radio stations** soon emerged in 1967 to break the BBC's monopoly.

Types of music stations

There are five major types of music radio stations in Australia today. The most common are classified as Classic Hits/Gold, which means they play music from the 1960s, 1970s and 1980s. The other categories of music stations are: Contemporary, Easy Listening, Country and Classical. Contemporary stations play the latest releases. Easy Listening stations play well-known songs and tunes aimed at an older audience. Country stations play country and western music and are particularly popular in regional Australia. Classical stations play classical music. Some community radio stations play more alternative contemporary music.

The disc jockey

The person who plays and announces songs is known as a disc jockey. This term originated in America in the late 1940s. In the early days of rock music, disc jockeys held a lot of power because they decided which records to play. This led to a practice known as **payola**, which was particularly common in America. It involved record companies offering money and gifts to disc jockeys in return for playing their records.

Today, disc jockeys do not choose which records to play. The stations have a **playlist** that contains a list of songs that have to be played. Having a playlist means that listeners are likely to hear their favourite songs no matter which disc jockey is on duty. In Australia, one aspect that radio stations have to consider when making up the playlist is that a certain number of songs played must be by Australian artists.

Before computerised song selection, music was played on record players by disc jockeys.

Technological advances

The evolution of radio and music technology has seen major changes to the way music is played by radio stations. Vinyl records made way for cassette and **reel-to-reel** tapes, which in turn made way for compact discs. Now, most modern radio stations use a computer to play music. All the songs on a radio station's playlist are stored on a computer, and when the name of a particular song is selected, it plays automatically. This means that records, tapes and CDs are no longer seen in many radio station studios.

Promoting Australia

Music stations in Australia are required to play a certain amount of music by Australian artists. This is to protect and promote the Australian music industry. Radio stations playing the latest hits have to ensure that at least 25 per cent of songs played are by Australian artists. Classic Hits/Gold stations and News/Talk stations have to play at least 15 per cent of songs by Australian artists. For Easy Listening and Country stations, the figure is 10 per cent, and stations playing jazz music only have to reach the figure of 5 per cent.

Breakfast Radio

More people listen to the radio at breakfast time than at any other time during the day. People listen to the radio when they wake up, when they have breakfast, when they get ready to leave home for work or school, and in the car. Because so many people listen to the radio in the morning, radio stations can charge advertisers more to advertise at this time than at any other time. This means the breakfast slot is the most competitive of all. Another reason that radio stations put a great deal of effort into capturing listeners at breakfast time, is that once a listener is tuned into a radio station, they are less likely to switch to another station later in the day.

Breakfast radio has not always been the most popular slot. Before television, the radio set was a family's evening entertainment. Only when most households had obtained television sets and began watching television programs after dinner did breakfast time become so important to radio station managers.

Range of programs

In Australia, there is a wide range of programs at breakfast time. Some concentrate on presenting news and current affairs, and inform people about what has happened around the world

Essential to breakfast

The three elements that almost all morning shows have in common are: regular weather reports, traffic reports and time calls. Informing listeners about the weather helps them work out what type of clothes to wear. By broadcasting traffic reports, radio stations are likely to keep people listening when they've left home and are travelling in their car. Giving regular time calls enables listeners to know whether they are running late or are on time.

overnight and what major events people can expect to take place in Australia throughout the day. Others play music, although the type of music differs from that played later in the day. In the morning, the music needs to be lively, to help wake people up and get them ready for the day.

One of the most popular breakfast formats is a mix of comedy and music. In recent years, radio stations have hired well-known comedians to present breakfast radio shows. Most of them have had little previous experience on radio but have become popular on television or through the **stand-up comedy** circuit.

One of Australia's well-known breakfast radio personalities—Andrew Denton.

Some of the most successful have been Wendy Harmer, Richard Stubbs, Andrew Denton, Tony Martin and Mick Molloy.

Competitions and give-aways

The marketing departments of radio stations are constantly trying to think of new ways to attract listeners to the breakfast shows. Competitions and give-aways are more common in breakfast shows than in any other show during the day.

Talk-back **Radio**

Growth of talk-back radio

One type of radio program that has been popular in Australia since the mid-1960s is talk-back radio. Like many aspects of Australian culture, it originated in America. Before 1967, talk-back radio did not exist in Australia in the way that it does now. Radio stations were not allowed to broadcast listeners' calls live to air. This is because government regulations restricted the way telephones could be used. Talk-back shows did exist, but they had to be recorded and edited before going to air.

In 1967, the Australian government lifted its restrictions, and talk-back radio began in the form we now know it. Several features were put in place to stop offensive comments going to air.

They included a seven-second delay, which meant that what listeners heard had actually been said seven seconds earlier, and a panic button, which when pressed beeped out offensive words. These measures are still in place today.

The radio industry quickly realised that it was the perfect medium for a talk-back format. It gave listeners the opportunity to participate directly in discussions about any topic. Several television stations have tried to adapt the talk-back formula but without much success.

Talk-back radio host in Melbourne, Jon Faine.

Talk-back personality, John Laws.

Talk-back hosts

Talk-back radio hosts have a great deal of power. They can express their own views on particular subjects, can hang up on callers they disagree with and have calls screened so that only callers with particular views are aired. However, the talk-back hosts like to hear from people with differing views and will often provoke arguments. They know that conflict attracts more listeners.

Talk-back and politicians

Politicians have a love/hate relationship with talk-back radio. They realise that talk-back programs give them the opportunity to get their views across to a large number of voters. But it also means that regular people can ring up and ask embarrassing questions. During elections, political parties arrange for their supporters to ring up politicians. If the politicians are from their side of politics, the caller will try to make the politician appear clever. If the politician is from a different party, they will try to embarrass them.

There have been several very successful talk-back hosts over the years. The most famous is the controversial John Laws who started off as a regular disc jockey but quickly realised how popular talk-back radio was going to become. Other successful talk-back hosts have been John Pearce and Alan Jones in Sydney, Jon Faine and Neil Mitchell in Melbourne, Howard Sattler in Perth and Jeremy Cordeaux in Adelaide.

Sport on Radio

Australia is a sport-loving nation, and many of Australia's greatest sporting triumphs have been broadcast on radio. Before television, families sat around the radio listening to cricket tests, Davis Cup tennis matches, boxing bouts and many other sporting contests around the world that involved Australians.

Attempts to prevent broadcasting of sport

In the 1930s, when sports broadcasting on radio began, many sporting associations and clubs did everything they could to stop radio stations broadcasting events live. They felt that if people could stay at home and listen, they would not spend money to attend the contest. Horse-racing broadcasters came up with new and different ways to call the races. They would climb trees or ladders alongside the racetracks, or stand on the top of trucks parked outside. Race club officials would respond by putting obstacles in the way or sending people out to chop the trees down. One race-caller outsmarted a club by hiring a hot-air balloon and floating above the racetrack while calling the races.

The first live calls of cricket tests from England were really broadcast from a studio in Sydney. The information about the game would be sent by **cable** from England to the studio, where commentators sat around a table relaying the information as if they were at the ground. A **sound effects** person played a record of a crowd cheering at the appropriate moments, and the sound of the ball hitting the bat was replicated by one of the commentators tapping a pencil against a piece of wood. All the time, the listeners were under the impression that the call was coming directly from the cricket ground.

Replicating the cricket: a broadcast of a cricket test in the 1930s.

Today

Today, weekend radio broadcasting is dominated by sport on both commercial and the ABC stations. Sporting clubs' concern that listening to events on radio would stop people attending was transferred to television. In fact, many people attending sporting events take along a radio to listen to while they watch. Hundreds of horse races and virtually every major Australian football, rugby league and cricket match can be heard live every week.

Left at the start

One of the hardest horse races for a race-caller to broadcast is a long-distance jumping race called the Warrnambool Grand Annual Steeplechase. Race-caller Bert Bryant put a lot of effort into his first call of this race. With comments before and after the race, and the call of the long race, he was on air for some twelve minutes. Or so he thought. Exhausted, he was not in the best mood when he discovered his microphone had not been turned on and no-one had heard a word he said!

23

Advertising on Radio

Without advertising, most radio stations would not exist. Playing advertisements is how they make enough money to pay their staff and broadcast programs. The exception are government-funded radio stations, such as those run by the ABC, and public radio stations, which depend on donations.

The first radio advertisement in the world was broadcast on an American station in 1923. It cost the company fifty dollars and resulted in sales of their product of $27 000. Australia's first radio advertisements were probably broadcast on 2UE in 1925.

Early days

In the early days, most radio station executives treated advertising on radio similar to how advertising in newspapers is treated. They charged per word, rather than by time as is the case now. A lot of advertising revenue came from companies sponsoring entire shows rather than advertisements played during a break. In fact, most popular shows included the sponsor's name in the title. There was the Lux Radio Theatre, Caltex Theatre, General Motors Hour and Mobil Quest. In some cases, a company would approach a radio station with an idea for a show they wished to sponsor and that is how many new programs started out.

Prices paid

The price a radio station charges advertisers has always depended on a program's ratings. It is more expensive to have an advertisement aired during a popular program than during one with fewer listeners. That is why radio station executives place a lot of importance on their programs' ratings. If not many people are listening to a particular program, they have to make changes, otherwise advertisers will take their business elsewhere.

The new radio drama *When A Girl Marries* has thousands of dedicated fans

Presenting RADIOS MOST APPEALING HUMAN INTEREST ROMANCE

"WHEN A GIRL MARRIES"

2CH MONDAY TO THURSDAY 7·15 P.M.

featuring RON RANDELL and MARIE CLARKE

SPONSORED BY THE MFRS OF.....

MORTEIN Insect Spray ε

This advertisement was for a radio program sponsored by a fly spray company.

Different ways

There are many different ways to advertise on radio. The most common is to have an advertisement made, using writers and actors, then have it played during an advertisement break. Other ways include paying a broadcaster to mention a product or company, or sponsoring a particular segment or show. A company might try all three ways to test which is the most effective.

Paying attention

Do you listen to advertisements on the radio or do you tune out until the next song comes on? Well, it is the job of a copywriter to make sure you pay attention to an advertisement. To do that, they may make the advertisements funny or have a familiar tune playing in the background. They may hire someone famous to read from a script or use cartoon character voices. Next time you hear a radio advertisement, pay attention to how the writer is trying to keep you listening.

Legends of Australian Radio

Many people have contributed to the success of Australian radio. Probably the most influential was Ernest Fisk who came to Australia from England in 1911 to open a branch of the Marconi Company. He demonstrated the new medium of radio to Australians and became chairman of AWA, Australia's most important and largest radio broadcasting company.

Charles Moses was another important administrator. He began his career as a broadcaster but served as general manager of the ABC from 1935 to 1965.

Radio legend, Jack Davey (right).

Quiz show hosts

Before television came along, the most popular stars of radio were actors and quiz show hosts. The kings of quiz were undoubtedly Bob Dyer and Jack Davey. Dyer was born in America and settled in Australia in the late 1930s. He hosted "The Bob Dyer Show", "Can You Take It?" and "Pick-a-Box". "Pick-a-Box" later ran for many years on television. Davey was a New Zealander and hosted a number of quiz shows sponsored by Colgate-Palmolive. Unlike Dyer, Davey failed to succeed on television.

Actors

Three of the most popular radio drama actors were women: Queenie Ashton, Lyndall Barbour and Gwen Plumb. Ashton's most famous role was as Granny Bishop in "Blue Hills". "Blue Hills" ran for twenty-seven years and was written by Gwen Meredith, one of Australia's most successful radio drama writers. Barbour played the role of Portia in "Portia Faces Life" from 1952 to 1970. Gwen Plumb had success as both an actor and a presenter of programs for women.

Radio legend, Queenie Ashton.

Comedians

Undoubtedly the most successful radio comedians were Roy Rene and George Wallace. They performed together on the **vaudeville** circuit for many years but split up before moving to radio. Both then had their own successful radio shows.

Presenters

Since the introduction of television, it has been the presenters who have become the stars of radio. Of the many presenters over the years, the most popular and successful have been Melbourne's Norman Banks, Peter Evans and Derryn Hinch, and Sydney's John Laws and Gary O'Callaghan.

A Day in the Life of a Radio Station

5:00 A.M.
Preparation is under way for the breakfast show. First news bulletin is being written. Overnight presenter is on air.

6:00 A.M.
First news bulletin of the day is read. Breakfast presenter prepares to go to air. Producer makes a final check of the show's running sheet.

7:30 A.M.
Breakfast presenter is in full swing. Producer copes with last-minute changes and puts listeners' calls through to presenter. Journalists begin making telephone calls to get a response from those in the news.

8:00 A.M.
Another news bulletin. Breakfast presenter and producer discuss how the show is going. News director briefs journalists as to which stories they should chase up during the day. Producer and presenter of morning show discuss the show's content and finalise the running order.

9:00 A.M.
Breakfast show ends, morning show begins. Journalists are on the road chasing up stories. Station manager deals with day-to-day running of the station, all the while keeping an ear on what is being broadcast.

11:00 A.M.
Morning show in full swing. Journalists ring in with news stories for midday bulletin. Breakfast show producer and presenter discuss likely stories for tomorrow's show and prepare preliminary running sheet.

11:30 A.M.
News editors edit tapes of journalists' stories in preparation for midday news.

Noon

Major news bulletin. Morning presenter leaves studio to be replaced by afternoon show host. Producers also swap over in the control room.

1:00 P.M.

Breakfast show presenter leaves the station, although producer still has some work to do to prepare for next day's show. Morning show staff discuss how their show went and begin preparing for the next day's show. Evening show producer starts work.

4:00 P.M.

Afternoon show finishes. Drive show begins. Journalists file final stories for the day. Evening show presenter arrives.

6:00 P.M.

Drive show finishes. Last major news bulletin of the day, then evening show begins.

Midnight

Overnight show begins. Presenter is all alone to take phone calls, play music and advertisements and make coffee.

4:30 A.M.

First news room and breakfast show staff arrive for a new day.

Neil Mitchell, a well-known talk-back host in Melbourne.

Timeline

1864 — James Clerk Maxwell produces mathematical evidence that radio waves exist.

1888 — Heinrich Hertz produces physical evidence proving Maxwell's theory.

1895 — Guglielmo Marconi sends a message using radio waves.

1897 — Professor William Bragg demonstrates Marconi's radio technology in Adelaide.

1901 — Guglielmo Marconi sends a message across the Atlantic Ocean.

1902 — John Ambrose Fleming invents the **diode valve**.

1906 — Reginald A. Fessenden becomes the first person to have his voice broadcast over radio.

1907 — Lee De Forest invents the **triode**.

1923–1927 — First official Australian radio broadcasts begin.

1932 — ABC begins radio transmission. Radio surveys are first used in Australia.

1933 — FM radio broadcasting is developed by Edwin Armstrong.

1948 — Transistor radios are invented.

1969 — Radio signals carry Neil Armstrong's words from the Moon to Earth.

1980 — First Australian commercial FM radio station begins operation.

2001 — Digital radio is introduced in Australia.

Glossary

AM amplitude modulation; a method of broadcasting that involves altering the height of the radio waves

cable a message sent long distances through a network of underwater wires

call-sign a short tune that lets listeners know which radio station they are listening to

copywriter a writer who specialises in writing short, snappy items, usually for advertising purposes

digital radio will offer CD quality sound, and pictures and text messages on an inbuilt screen

diode valve a device that helps to receive radio waves

electrical current a flow of electricity

FM frequency modulation; a method of broadcasting that involves altering the distance between each radio wave

frequency the number of cycles in a radio wave. Changing the dial on a radio results in the radio picking up waves of different frequencies.

Morse Code a system of sending messages in which letters and numbers are replaced by various combinations of taps, dots and dashes

payola illegally receiving a gift for promoting something

pirate radio station an illegal radio station

playlist a list of songs that a radio station plays

ratings a system that determines how many people are listening to a radio station at any one time

receiver a device that translates the radio wave back into the sound it originally was

reel-to-reel a tape recorder that uses large rolls of tape rather than a cassette

regional outside the major cities

running sheet the list of items, guests and segments to appear on a show

segment a portion or section

sound effects sounds other than speech or music manufactured by artificial means

stand-up comedy a form of performance where comedians appear before a live audience

subscription paying for the privilege of viewing or receiving something regularly

transmitter a device used to send a radio wave to its destination

triode a device that helps send radio signals further distances

vaudeville a form of entertainment featuring variety acts

voice-over artist a person whose voice (but not face) is used to explain or promote something

volunteer a worker who receives no money for the job they do

warrant written authorisation or permission to carry something out

Further Information

Books

Broadcasting in Australia. Australian Broadcasting Tribunal, Sydney, 1992.
Children's Britannica, Vol 14. Encyclopedia Britannica Inc, London, 1993.
Collier's Encyclopedia, Vol 19. P. F. Collier Inc, New York, Toronto, Sydney, 1993.
Crystal, D. (ed). *Cambridge Biographical Encyclopedia*. Cambridge University Press, Cambridge, 1994.
How Is It Done? Reader's Digest Association Ltd, London, 1990.
Macmillan Science & Technology Encyclopedia, Vol 9. Macmillan Education Australia, Melbourne, 1992.
Self, D. *Media Focus – Radio.* Heinemann Library, Oxford, 1998.

Websites

http://www.asap.unimelb.edu.au/hstm/hstm_communications.htm – for information on Marconi, and the invention of the radio.
http://www.aba.gov.au/ – Australian Broadcasting Authority. This site has information on all the radio and television stations in Australia.

Index